Exceptional
African Americans

CRISPUS ATTUCKS

A Hero of the American Revolution

Charlotte Taylor

Enslow Publishing
101 W. 23rd Street
Suite 240
New York, NY 10011
USA
enslow.com

Words to Know

announcement—Something that is stated officially or publicly.

colony—An area that is ruled by another country.

courage—Bravery or fearlessness.

harpoon—A long weapon often used to hunt large fish or whales.

independence—Freedom from the control of others.

injustice—An unfair act.

massacre—The cruel killing of many people.

musket—A gun with a long barrel that was used before the rifle was invented.

slave—Someone is owned by another person and thought of as property.

stray—To wander away or get lost.

Contents

Crispus Attucks

CHAPTER 1

A Dream of Freedom

Crispus Attucks was born a **slave** in 1723. He and his family lived on a large farm in Framingham, Massachusetts. His father, Prince, had been captured in Africa. He was brought to the **colonies** on a ship and sold as a slave. Nancy, Crispus's mother, was a member of the Natick Indian tribe. Crispus also had an older sister, Phebe. The family worked for their master, Colonel Buckminster.

By the time he was a teenager, Crispus wanted to be free. He did not like the idea of being owned. Crispus dreamed of becoming a sailor. But Colonel

Naught but a slave was Attucks, And yet how grand a hero, too.

-Olivia Bush, "Crispus Attucks"

In the 1700s, slavery was legal in all of the colonies. Slaves were brought from Africa on ships to work in fields as well as in homes.

Buckminster had no ships. Later, Crispus was sold to a new master named William Brown. He moved to Boston near the shipping docks.

A New Life

William Brown taught Crispus the cattle business. He bought and sold cattle for his master. Crispus became very good at his new trade. But his dreams of becoming a free man had not died. Crispus did not like that black people were forced into slavery. He wanted to be free and become a sailor.

Crispus may have gone to markets like this one to buy and sell cattle when he worked for William Brown.

CHAPTER 2

Crispus Escapes

The Boston Harbor was full of ships. Crispus watched them coming and going. Soon he was able to spot a **stray** ship. It was a whaling ship. One night William Brown was away. Crispus slipped away to talk to the captain. The captain liked that Crispus was a big, strong man. The captain hired him that night.

Crispus went below deck to hide. He worried that he might be captured before the ship left port. The ship sailed out to sea the next morning. Crispus's dreams were coming true.

The Boston Harbor was a very busy seaport. Crispus was able to escape slavery by working on the ships that came into the harbor.

Soon William Brown discovered that Crispus had run away. On October 2, 1750, Brown placed an **announcement** in a newspaper called the *Boston Gazette*. It stated that Crispus Attucks was a runaway slave. From then on, Crispus always had to be careful. If he was caught, he would lose his newfound freedom.

Life at Sea

For the next twenty years, Crispus worked on ships at sea. He learned to hunt and catch whales. Work on whaling ships was dangerous. Crispus learned to throw a **harpoon**. In those days, whales were worth a lot of money. Whale blubber, or fat, was turned into oil for burning in lamps.

Crispus worked on a whaling ship like this one. It was hard, dangerous work. Many sailors lost their lives at sea.

For our freedom now and forever,
his head was the first bid low.

–John Boyle O'Reilly, "Crispus Attucks"

Crispus had to be very careful everywhere he went. Slave catchers were paid to find runaway slaves and return them to their masters. This drawing shows a fight between a group of slaves and slave catchers.

Sailors like Crispus killed whales with harpoons. The whale blubber could be used for candles and lamps.

Whaling captains valued Crispus's hard work and **courage**. He missed his family, though. He was at sea most of the year. Sometimes the ship returned to Boston. At these times, Crispus secretly visited his family. Luckily, he was never caught.

CHAPTER 3

Trouble in the Colonies

The American colonies were ruled by Great Britain. By the 1760s, many colonists wanted **independence**. They wanted to be able to make their own laws. They did not want to pay taxes to the king in England. As the years went on, their need for freedom grew stronger.

King George of England did not like the idea of American independence. In 1769 he sent about a thousand British soldiers to Boston. He hoped the troops would calm the colonists. Instead, the arrival of the soldiers made the colonists more upset. Life was uneasy between the British and the colonists.

A Need for Independence

Crispus continued to work on whalers. He often heard about the trouble in the colonies. He understood their strong need for independence. He had been working and hiding for his own freedom. Crispus wanted to help the colonists. But he feared being captured and returned to slavery.

Call it riot or revolution, his hand first clenched at the crown; His feet were the first in perilous place to pull the king's flag down.

-John Boyle O'Reilly, "Crispus Attucks"

King George did not want the colonies to be independent. Many people in England agreed with him.

Colonists were angry because they had to pay a great deal of money to England. Here a group of people in Boston read an announcement about new taxes.

CHAPTER 4
One Deadly Night

In the early months of 1770, there were some small fights between the colonists and the British soldiers. But on the evening of March 5, 1770, the trouble grew. A colonist had done some work for a British soldier that night. The soldier refused to pay him. Quickly, news spread through Boston of this **injustice**.

Colonists gathered in the streets. They yelled and threw snowballs and rocks at the British soldiers. The soldiers fought back. The soldiers hit colonists with sticks and the tips of their **muskets**. Crispus was in Boston that night. He bravely joined his fellow colonists.

An End and a Beginning

Crispus fought alongside white colonists against the British soldiers. But he did not care about the color of the colonists' skin. The fight for freedom was more

The just man shall be in eternal remembrance

The brave Soldier of the Revolutionary War 1770.

Crispus spent long periods of time at sea. But he happened to be visiting Boston on the evening of March 5, 1770.

In this drawing of the Boston Massacre, Crispus can be seen being hit by a bullet. He was the first to die that night.

important to him. A big fight broke out on King Street in front of the Customs House. Crispus tried to grab a musket from one of the soldiers.

A British soldier shot and killed Crispus. Four other colonists were killed that night. Crispus Attucks was one of the first people to give his life for American independence.

> **Then write in glowing letters**
> **These thrilling words in history,—**
> **That Attucks was a hero,**
> **That Attucks died for Liberty.**
> **—Oliva Bush, "Crispus Attucks"**

The Boston **Massacre** led to the Revolutionary War. The colonists won the war and became independent from Britain's rule. Crispus gave his life to help free the very colonists who had once made him a slave.

Crispus Attucks lost his life in the Boston Massacre fighting for America's freedom.

Timeline

1723—Crispus Attucks is born a slave in Framingham, Massachusetts.

1750—Crispus runs away to become a sailor.

1750–1770—Crispus works on a whaling ship.

1770—Crispus is one of the first men killed in the fight for American independence. This event became known as the Boston Massacre.

Learn More

Books

Rajczak, Kristen. *Life During the American Revolution*. New York: Gareth Stevens, 2013.

Shea, Therese. *The Boston Massacre*. New York: Gareth Stevens, 2014.

Weiss, Lynne. *Crispus Attucks and the Boston Massacre*. New York: PowerKids Press, 2013.

Websites

www.ducksters.com/history/colonial_america/slavery.php
Explains the history of slavery in Colonial America, including the slaves' daily lives and their treatment.

www.landofthebrave.info/boston-massacre.htm
Learn about the circumstances leading up to the Boston Massacre as well as details of the event itself and what happened afterward.

Index

Published in 2016 by Enslow Publishing, LLC.
101 W. 23rd Street, Suite 240, New York, NY 10011

Copyright © 2016 by Enslow Publishing, LLC.

Library of Congress Cataloging-in-Publication Data
Taylor, Charlotte, 1978- author.
Crispus Attucks : a hero of the American Revolution / Charlotte Taylor.
    pages cm. — (Exceptional African Americans)
Includes bibliographical references and index.
Summary: "Describes the life and contributions of Crispus Attucks during the American Revolution"— Provided by publisher.
Audience: Grades 4 to 6.
ISBN 978-0-7660-7187-2 (library binding)
ISBN 978-0-7660-7185-8 (pbk.)
ISBN 978-0-7660-7186-5 (6-pack)
1. Attucks, Crispus, -1770—Juvenile literature. 2. African Americans—Biography—Juvenile literature. 3. Revolutionaries—Massachusetts—Boston—Biography—Juvenile literature. 4. Boston Massacre, 1770—Juvenile literature. I. Title.
E185.97.A86T39 2016
973.3'113092—dc23
[B]
                    2015026936

Printed in the United States of America

To Our Readers: We have done our best to make sure all website addresses in this book were active and appropriate when we went to press. However, the author and the publisher have no control over and assume no liability for the material available on those websites or on any websites they may link to. Any comments or suggestions can be sent by e-mail to customerservice@enslow.com.

Poetry Excerpts: pp. 11, 16, John Boyle O'Reilly, "Crispus Attucks," Crispus Attucks Museum, 2015, http://www.crispusattucksmuseum.org/crispus-attucks-poem/; pp. 6, 20, Olivia Bush, "Crispus Attucks," *Original Poems* (Providence, R.I.: Press of Louis A. Basinet, 1899).

Photo Credits: Throughout book, ©Toria/Shutterstock.com (blue background); cover, pp. 1, 4 Archive Photos/Getty Images; p. 6 Hulton Archive/Getty Images; p. 7 Art Media/Print Collector/Hulton Fine Art Collection/Getty Images; p. 9 John Carwitham/BPL/Boston ca 1723/Creative Commons Attribution 2.0 Generic license; p. 10 SSPL/Getty Images; pp. 11, 18, Library of Congress Prints & Photographs Division; p. 12 © North Wind Picture Archives; p. 15 DeAgostini/Getty Images; p. 16 Universal History Archive/ UIG/Getty Images; p. 19 National Archives Catalogue; p. 21 Prisma/UIG/Getty Images.